ANIMAL SAFARI

Tree Frogs

by Chris Bowman

BELLWETHER MEDIA • MINNEAPOLIS, MN

Note to Librarians, Teachers, and Parents:

Blastoff! Readers are carefully developed by literacy experts and combine standards-based content with developmentally appropriate text.

Level 1 provides the most support through repetition of high-frequency words, light text, predictable sentence patterns, and strong visual support.

Level 2 offers early readers a bit more challenge through varied simple sentences, increased text load, and less repetition of high-frequency words.

Level 3 advances early-fluent readers toward fluency through increased text and concept load, less reliance on visuals, longer sentences, and more literary language.

Level 4 builds reading stamina by providing more text per page, increased use of punctuation, greater variation in sentence patterns, and increasingly challenging vocabulary.

Level 5 encourages children to move from "learning to read" to "reading to learn" by providing even more text, varied writing styles, and less familiar topics.

Whichever book is right for your reader, Blastoff! Readers are the perfect books to build confidence and encourage a love of reading that will last a lifetime!

This edition first published in 2015 by Bellwether Media, Inc.

No part of this publication may be reproduced in whole or in part without written permission of the publisher. For information regarding permission, write to Bellwether Media, Inc., Attention: Permissions Department, 5357 Penn Avenue South, Minneapolis, MN 55419.

Library of Congress Cataloging-in-Publication Data

Bowman, Chris, 1990- author.
  Tree Frogs / by Chris Bowman.
    pages cm. – (Blastoff! Readers. Animal Safari)
  Includes bibliographical references and index.
  Summary: "Developed by literacy experts for students in kindergarten through grade three, this book introduces tree frogs to young readers through leveled text and related photos"– Provided by publisher.
  Audience: Ages 5-8.
  Audience: K to grade 3.
  ISBN 978-1-62617-166-4 (hardcover : alk. paper)
  1. Hylidae–Juvenile literature. 2. Frogs–Juvenile literature. [1. Tree frogs.] I. Title. II. Series: Blastoff! Readers. 1, Animal Safari.
  QL668.E24B69 2015
  597.87'8–dc23
                                                                          2014034752

Printed in the United States of America, North Mankato, MN.

Contents

What Are Tree Frogs?

Tree frogs are small **amphibians**. They are found all around the world.

Tree frogs live in forests, grasslands, and **rain forests**. They stay close to water.

Climbers

Most tree frogs stay high up in trees. Some live under wet leaves or grasses.

All tree frogs can climb. Their toes have sticky **pads**. They help the frogs **grip** branches.

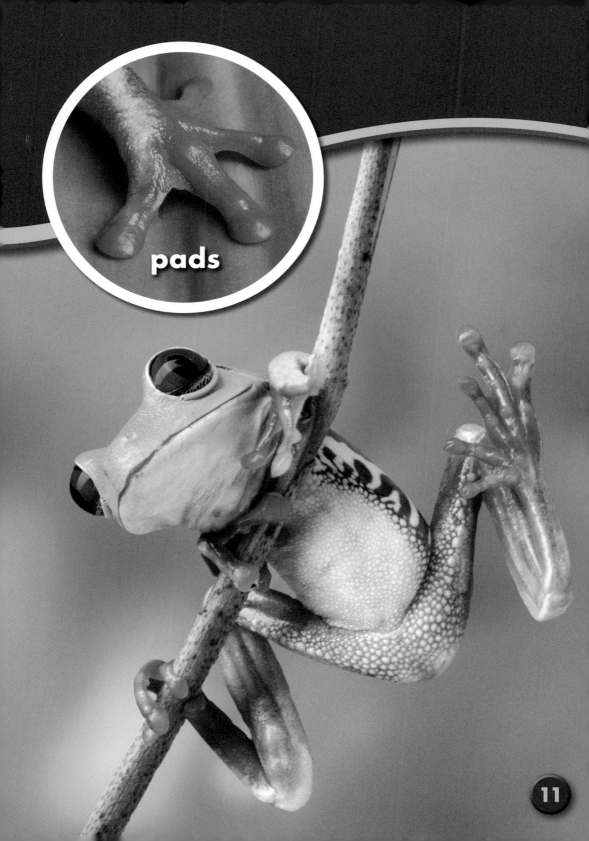

pads

Hunting and Hiding

Tree frogs hunt for **prey** at night. They catch moths, crickets, and flies.

They use their colors to hide from **predators**. Some have red eyes to surprise birds and snakes.

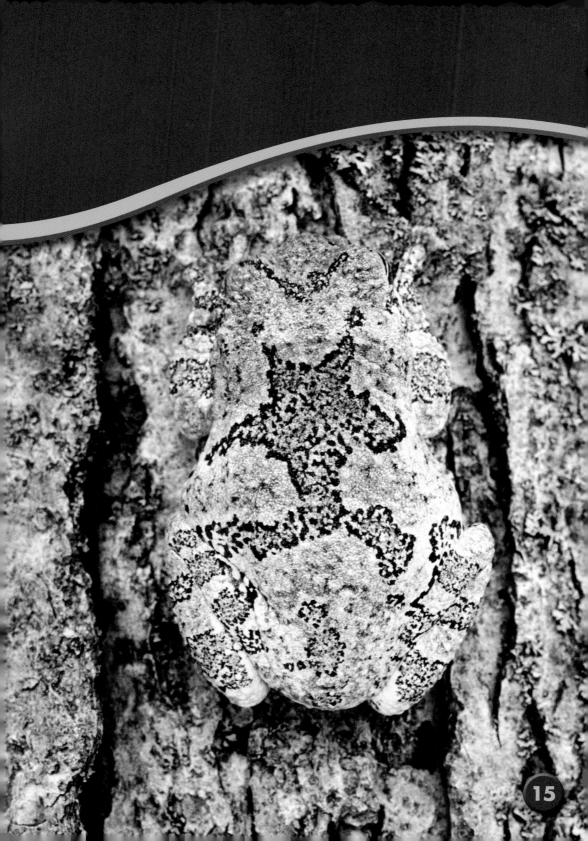

Males, Females, and Babies

Male tree frogs call to females. Their throats **inflate** like balloons.

Females lay eggs in or by water. **Tadpoles** break out of the eggs.

First they have
gills and tails.
Soon they grow
legs. Time to climb!

Glossary

amphibians—animals that live both on land and in water

gills—body parts that let animals breathe underwater

grip—to hold tightly

inflate—to blow up with air

pads—sticky parts on a tree frog's toes that help with climbing

predators—animals that hunt other animals for food

prey—animals that are hunted by other animals for food

rain forests—warm forests that receive a lot of rain

tadpoles—young frogs

To Learn More

AT THE LIBRARY

Green, Emily. *Frogs*. Minneapolis, Minn.: Bellwether Media, 2011.

Phillips, Dee. *Tree Frog*. New York, N.Y.: Bearport Pub., 2014.

Schuh, Mari. *Tree Frogs*. Minneapolis, Minn.: Jump!, 2015.

ON THE WEB

Learning more about tree frogs is as easy as 1, 2, 3.

1. Go to www.factsurfer.com.

2. Enter "tree frogs" into the search box.

3. Click the "Surf" button and you will see a list of related web sites.

With factsurfer.com, finding more information is just a click away.

Index

The images in this book are reproduced through the courtesy of: Dirk Ercken, front cover; Roger Meerts, p. 5; Emanuele Biggi/FLPA, p. 7 (top); StockThings, p. 7 (bottom left); biletskiy, p. 7 (bottom center); Andrzej Kubik, p. 7 (bottom right); masai, p. 9; Sascha Burkard, p. 11 (top); Artur Cupak/ Glow Images, p. 11 (bottom); Minden Pictures/ SuperStock, pp. 13 (top), 19; Rasmus Holmboe Dahl, p. 13 (bottom left); Yuangeng Zhang, p. 13 (bottom center); SweetCrisis, p. 13 (bottom right); Ethan Meleg/ SuperStock, p. 15; worldswildlifewonders, p. 17; Visuals Unlimited, Inc./ Thomas Marent/ Getty Images, p. 21.